YOUR KNOWLEDGE HAS VALUE

- We will publish your bachelor's and master's thesis, essays and papers

- Your own eBook and book - sold worldwide in all relevant shops

- Earn money with each sale

Upload your text at www.GRIN.com and publish for free

Bibliographic information published by the German National Library:

The German National Library lists this publication in the National Bibliography; detailed bibliographic data are available on the Internet at http://dnb.dnb.de .

This book is copyright material and must not be copied, reproduced, transferred, distributed, leased, licensed or publicly performed or used in any way except as specifically permitted in writing by the publishers, as allowed under the terms and conditions under which it was purchased or as strictly permitted by applicable copyright law. Any unauthorized distribution or use of this text may be a direct infringement of the author s and publisher s rights and those responsible may be liable in law accordingly.

Imprint:

Copyright © 2018 GRIN Verlag
Print and binding: Books on Demand GmbH, Norderstedt Germany
ISBN: 9783668639430

This book at GRIN:

https://www.grin.com/document/412793

G. V. Chandra Mouli

Influence of Individual Differences on Learning Attitudes

An Analysis of Personality Notion in Building Proactive Learning Organizations with Augmented Productivity

GRIN Verlag

GRIN - Your knowledge has value

Since its foundation in 1998, GRIN has specialized in publishing academic texts by students, college teachers and other academics as e-book and printed book. The website www.grin.com is an ideal platform for presenting term papers, final papers, scientific essays, dissertations and specialist books.

Visit us on the internet:

http://www.grin.com/

http://www.facebook.com/grincom

http://www.twitter.com/grin_com

Influence of Individual Differences on Learning Attitudes: An Analysis of Personality Notion in Building Proactive Learning Organizations with Augmented Productivity

Dr. G.V.Chandra Mouli, Head, Department of Business Administration, Sri Hari Degree & PG College, Kadapa, A.P. India.

Abstract

The Organizational Advancement lies with its proactive moves effectively designed and adopted. Organizations are operating in a dynamic environment where continuous improvements and developments are required in managing resources particularly the most valuable Human Resources. In this globalized era the organizations are expected to tackle different levels of competition presenting a new milieu for growth and survival. In simple, this process can be called as creating learning organizations. In workplace the individual differences play a crucial role, it is a universal fact that all humans are unique with their abilities, skills, knowledge; moreover differ in perceptions, attitudes towards job. Managing these set of variables is the required component to create improved learning organizations and productivity. Every individual perceives and understands the organizational goals, roles and work in their own way. These individual differences should be rightly lined with organizational goals. This paper emphasizes the impact and influence of individual differences on learning attitudes, which is allied with creating proactive learning organizations through individual learning with augmented productivity constituent.

Keywords: Organizational Progression, Human Resources, Individual Differences, Learning Organizations, Productivity.

- Introduction 3
- Learning Theories 4
- Personality and Learning Attitudes 4
- Significance of the study 5
- Objectives of the Study 5
- Hypothesis 6
- Methodology 6
- Analysis 6
- Major Findings 10
- Strategic Imperatives 11
- Scope for further Research 12
- Conclusion 13
- References 14

Introduction

Learning is defined as any relatively permanent change in behavior that occurs as a result of experience (Stephen p.robbins & Seema Sanghi, 2006). Organizations comprises of the unique individuals generally working in a collaborative milieu (Fred Luthans, 2003). The ultimate objective of any organization is reaching excellence benchmark; it is all about transformational process which consists of devising unique strategies, understanding dynamics of business environment, effective estimations towards competition levels and resource management (Westerman, J.W. & Simmons, B.L., 2007). Moreover it is a matter of learning, every move and action used by the organizations taught many lessons to the employees. The learning aspect delineates organization's progress towards successful transformations (Gumusluoglu, L., Ilsev, A., 2009). The existence of individual differences in the workplace is quiet common; they differ in many facets like personality, perceptions, attitudes, skills, abilities, attitudes, values, behaviors etc. These differences have strong influence on organizational advancement (Chamorro-Premuzic, T., & Reichenbacher, L., 2008). Individual's improvement in work related aspects which results in organizational development (Furnham, A., Batey, M., Anand, K., & Manfield, J., 2008). The application of creativity, novelty and inventions with regard to work procedural perfection lies with understanding personality factor of human resources (Aguilar-Alonso, A., 1996). There is a close relationship between personality and productivity; because human resources outcomes are linked with managing their behaviors and tuning as per the organizational requirements. In fact the personal improvements strongly associated with learning attitudes. The ever changing business environment presents many challenges in front of the organizations; its implications are more on organizational moves. The reality is that success depends on how effectively business houses are understands, absorbs, observes and devises their ways towards a prosperous future. All these collectively called as a proactive learning process may be individual or organizational perspective (Gerhardt, M., Bryan, A. & Newman, R.W., 2009). The individual differences among employees will effect on many behavioral and professional aspects (Chamorro-Premuzic, T., 2007). Due to these unmanaged personality differences adversely effects on the learning quotient. The personality traits influences individual performance at workplace i.e. the way behaviors displayed; In the recent times the most critical issue in front of the organizations is rightly accessing the impact of personality traits dynamics on individual performance (Dr.Y.Subbarayudu & G.V.Chandra Mouli, 2012). The personality competencies are enhanced due to experiencing new work allied methodologies, skill-gap analysis, adopting empathetic nature, knowing exactly how their valuable presence is highly solicited and reaching the state self-actualization. Today every organization wants to be called as a learning organization, because learning alone makes the difference, helps in gaining unique image in the competitive markets (Wagner, J.A, & Hollenbeck J.R., (1998). The organizations are always insists their human resources to come up with new ideas, called divergent thinking; a vital component to improve organizational productivity via individual progress which is associated with the managing personality (Furnham, A., Batey, M., Anand, K., & Manfield, J., 2008). The nature of human intelligence is completely unique, emotionally reactive and results in behavioral actions (Guilford, J. P., 1967). The actions of the human resources are the result of personality interaction with the environment.

Learning Theories

Learning concept can be understood clearly through studying the theories. The three theories which explain the term learning are Classical Conditioning (A type of conditioning in which an individual respondents to some stimulus that would not ordinarily produce such a response, Operant Conditioning (A type of conditioning in which desired voluntary behavior leads to a reward or prevents a punishment) and Social-Learning Theory (People can learn through observation and direct experience). The theoretical study concentrates more on three specific factors like situations, rewards, self experience. But anyhow here the individual observations and experience quotients are the base for learning. Working in collaborative environment is about presence of individuals with diversified personalities (Chauhan, D., & Chauhan, S., P., 2006). All these will results in individual differences. The role of individual differences in decision making is crucial and critical in nature. Decision making in practice is characterized by bounded rationality, common human biases and errors, and the use of intuition (Vincent, A., Decker, B., & Mumford, M., 2002). In addition, there are individual differences that create deviations due to many personality associated variables.

Personality and Learning Attitudes

The learning attitudes of internal customers are interlinked with personality facet. The workplace issues like recognition, reputation, individuality, openness to share ideas, views acceptance rate, past performance analysis, superior's observations, change management initiatives, motivation and fair treatment (R.N.Taylor and M.D.Dunnette, 1974). Ultimately all the above elements deeply related with personality notion i.e. individual differences. Every individual has their own way and approach to tackle workplace issues, but this may results in misunderstandings and misinterpretations which affects on productivity (Colquitt, J, Le-Pine, J, & Wesson, M., 2009). Personal interests, preferences and temperaments decide the proactive learning intuition. Creativity and Work Intelligence are the successful outcomes of precisely lined individual differences (Batey, M., & Furnham, A., 2006).

Generally learning is a experiencing process occurs due to situations, events happened, level of involvement, understanding, perception towards individual's influence in attaining goals, and realizing the collaborative efforts in reaching targets (Burke, L., A., & Witt, L., A., 2004). But already the organizations are recognized this as routine process, presents many questions with respect to the advanced learning behaviors including brainstorming (Bolin, A., U., & Neuman, G., A., 2006). The equations towards situations learning are drastically changed; today the organizations are busy in making their human resources to place in the arena of proactive learning environment (Gerhardt, M., Bryan, A. & Newman, R.W., 2009). Learning from the situations happened; market changes, strategies adopted and results gained is almost obsolete. So what is the solution? How? The answer may be re-engineering of organizational learning process. Top management designs strategies, middle and lower level implements those strategies, results in the form of organizational products and services, implications on the consumer or customer behavior; learning occurs at each and every stage of this process (Esque, T.J, & Gilmore, E.R., 2003). This is a causal learning scenario, required is proactive i.e. reversing the process learning from the customer or consumer, market environment, estimating organizational essentials with regard to gaining major market share, establishing a unique image among the minds of business parties, understanding need for valuable presence of self (employee), adopting the situational behavior as per organizational and individual needs (Davis Mkoji & Dr. Damary Sikalieh, 2012). The effective management of business dynamics lies with continuous internal improvement strategies organized and controlled. The productivity is only a quantitative measure to organization, depends on effective resource procurement and management. Productivity is coupled with continuous improvement philosophy; domino effect due to learning aspect. Is learning makes the difference! The answer may be again it's not about organizations but proactive human resources (Kim, T., Hon, A., & Crant, J. J., 2009). Enhanced productivity is one of the visible outcomes of managed individual differences at workplace.

Significance of the study

The study is intended to measure influence of individual differences on learning attitudes; its impression on creating proactive learning organizations with augmented productivity. Proactive Learning factor ensures enhanced organizational performance through effective human resource utilization which helps in reduced individual differences, rightly allied individual - organizational goals and managed personalities to tackle decisive concerns at workplace.

Objectives of the Study

The objectives of the study are:
1. To identify the influence of individual differences on organizational dynamics and various personal and organizational factors contributing to it;
2. To ascertain impact of individual differences on learning behaviors;
3. To assess the persuade of proactive learning attitudes of individuals on productivity and
4. To suggest strategic imperatives to enhance learning elasticity and establishing proactive learning organizations to improve productivity through managing individual differences.

Hypothesis

The following hypotheses are formulated in order to achieve the above objectives:
1. Unmanaged individual differences among human resources will have a negative impact on learning attitudes.
2. Proactive learning factor will results in enhanced productivity.
3. Managed personalities will have a positive impact on organizational innovations and
4. High consideration on lining individual differences will results in down to business transformations.
5.

Methodology

The purpose of this study is to examine how individual differences influence the organizational performance. A descriptive research design taking a survey approach is used. The target population of this study consisted of Software Engineers, Senior Software Engineers and Team Lead ranked employees of different IT Companies exist in International Tech Park Limited (ITPL), Bangalore, India. Judgmental Random Sampling procedure was followed to select sample respondents, looking into convenience 164 respondents are selected. Data is collected from the respondents by using the interview schedule specifically designed for the purpose. A non-probabilistic sampling method, namely convenience sampling is used in drawing samples for this study. The sample included 97 males (59.1%) and 67 (40.9%) females. The range of ages of the respondents is from 20 to 35 years. The educational level of the respondents is high with 87% holding bachelors or post graduate degrees. . Slightly more than half (52.8%) of the respondents reported that they hold the position of Software Engineers (Programmers); whereas 29.3% are Senior Software Engineers; and 17.9% Team Leaders. The survey was conducted from January 2013 to March 2013. The tabulated data is analyzed with various statistical tools like Mean, standard deviation, standard error, confidence interval, range, variance, kurtosis, skewness (Descriptive statistics), Pearson coefficient correlation (Association statistics) and Chi-square test (Frequency statistics).

Analysis

Table 1: Perception of the respondents towards individual differences

S.No.	Issue	Mean Score
1.	Individual differences is an emerging concern in modern organizations	18.2
2.	Successful Teams are the results depends on managing individual differences	21.4
3.	Understanding individual differences eliminates many job related issues	19.9
4.	Gender factor also affects on individual differences at workplace	22.4
5.	Organizational culture helps in lining individual differences	20.9
6.	Proactive personalities are the results of managed individual differences	18.7
7.	Learning attitudes are influenced by the personality factor	19.6
8.	Leadership impact on creating learning organizations is extreme	23.8

9.	Employee creativity lies with organizational-individual fit	17.2
10.	Enhanced productivity is the outcome of proactive learning	15.8

Source: primary data from field survey

From the above table 1 it is clear that greatest agreement is there for the issue 'Extreme impact of leadership on creating learning organizations (23.8 mean score); Gender factor affects on individual differences at workplace (22.4 mean score), Successful teams can be created through managing individual differences (21.4 mean score), Organizational culture assists in lining individual differences (20.9 mean score), understanding job related personality issues (19.9 mean score), Personality influence on learning attitudes (19.6 mean score), Proactive Personalities (18.7 mean score), Individual differences as an emerging concern (18.2 mean score), Employee creativity (17.2 mean score) and Enhanced productivity based on proactive learning (15.8 mean score);

Table 2: Influence of individual differences on learning behaviors

Concern	N	Mean	Variance	S.D	S.E
Process improvement	164	18.78	31.44	5.61	1.144633
Self-monitoring	164	19.11	40.11	6.33	1.156303
Goal-assessment	164	17.00	28.50	5.39	1.60963
Role clarity	164	17.11	26.36	5.13	1.548052
Team efficacy	164	20.33	45.75	6.76	1.640481
Individual Perceptions	164	19.78	55.19	7.42	1.801869

Source: Primary data from field survey

Table 2 visibly shows the mean ratings and standard deviations to the six factors for the whole sample. The Mean ranged from 17.00 to 20.33; Variance ranged from 26.36% to 55.19%; Standard Deviation ranged from 05.13 to 07.42 and Standard Error ranged from 1.144633 to 1.801869; As evidence by the mean ratings, the top learning behavior modulating is Team efficacy, it possesses the Highest Mean (20.33), Variance (45.45), Standard Deviation (12.26) and S.E (1.640481). This followed by Individual Perceptions towards work (with Mean (19.78), Variance (55.19), S.D (7.42) and S.E (1.801869); Self-monitoring (with Mean (19.11), Variance (40.11), S.D (6.33) and S.E (1.156303); Process Improvement (with Mean (18.78), Variance (31.44), S.D (5.61) and S.E (1.144633); Role clarity (with Mean (17.11), Variance (26.36), S.D (5.13) and S.E (1.548052) and Goal-assessment(with Mean (17.00), Variance (28.50), S.D (5.39) and S.E (1.60963);

Table 3: Impact of the personality dynamics on improved employee performance

Factor 95%CI	Mean	S.D	Kurtosis	Skewness	
Work Environment	22.4	11.53	-0.20598	0.906518	7.146033
Leadership	20.5	12.60	-0.33752	1.013296	7.808488
Appraisal Mechanism	23.1	11.83	-0.73057	0.587961	7.330312
Communication Levels	19.1	10.26	-1.41099	0.331132	6.357391
Values and perceptions	17.0	09.19	-0.34606	0.789313	5.695523
Intuition	21.2	11.74	-0.61669	0.886394	7.273905
Divergent Thinking	18.9	08.90	-0.13866	0.984041	5.516214
Self-esteem	21.9	13.29	0.727728	1.213999	8.235218
Competition Acceptance	25.1	14.19	-0.9884	0.653961	8.796578
Impression Management	22.5	11.19	-0.64707	0.69269	6.934137

Source: Primary data from field survey

Note: The value of 0.05 is used to give the 95% (0.95) confidence interval. The upper and lower ranges for the data are 32 and 14.

Table 3 reveals Mean and Standard deviations to the above mentioned factors for the whole sample. The S.D ranged from 17.0 to 25.1; Standard Deviation ranged from 8.90 to 14.19. The high influencing personality factors on improved employee performance are Competition acceptance (with Mean 25.1, S.D 14.19, Kurtosis -0.9884 and Skewness 0.653961), Appraisal Mechanism (with Mean 23.1, S.D 11.83, Kurtosis -0.73057 and Skewness 0.587961); Impression management (with Mean 22.5, S.D 11.19, Kurtosis -6.4707 and Skewness 0.69269); Work environment (with Mean 22.4, S.D 11.53, Kurtosis -0.20598 and Skewness 0.906518); and followed by Self-esteem (with Mean 21.9, S.D 13.29, Kurtosis 0.727728 and Skewness 1.213999); Intuition (with Mean 21.2, S.D 11.74, Kurtosis -0.61669 and Skewness 0.886394); Leadership (with Mean 20.5, S.D 12.60, Kurtosis -0.33752 and Skewness 1.013296); Communication levels (with Mean 19.1, S.D 10.26, Kurtosis -1.41099 and Skewness 0.331132);

Divergent thinking (with Mean 18.9, S.D 08.90, Kurtosis -0.13866 and Skewness 0.984041); Values and perceptions (with Mean 17.0, S.D 09.19, Kurtosis -0.34606 and Skewness 0.789313);

Table 4: Impression of Personality Notion on Proactive Learning Attitudes

Respondents	Observed Count	Expected Count
Team Leaders	30	29.5
Senior Software Engineers	47	51.4
Software Engineers	87	83.1
Total	164	164.00

Note: Specifically a simple Hypothesis designed. Null Hypothesis: Proactive Learning Attitudes are not influenced by the Personality Notion. Alternative Hypothesis: Proactive Learning Attitudes are influenced by the Personality Notion. Degrees of Freedom = (2-1) (2-1) =1, Calculated Value of χ^2 is 7.52706%, Tabulated Value of χ^2 for 1 Degree of Freedom=3.841.

Table 4 visibly shows that the calculated value of Chi-square (7.52706) is greater than tabulated value of Chi-square at 5% level of significance. Hence Null Hypothesis is rejected and proactive learning attitudes have been influenced by the personality factor.

Table 5: Managing Individual Differences V/s Developing Proactive Personalities
Pearson Correlation Coeffients

Personality Inkling	Factor 1	Factor 2	Factor 3	Factor 4	Factor 5
Functional behaviors	0.972188	0.962239	0.96182	0.990662	0.999923
Creativity at work	0.999814	0.978378	0.729995	+1	0.896166
Work autonomy	0.435932	0.876198	0.999751	0.178788	0.991175
Risk taking orientation	0.859104	0.983888	0.475769	0.78868	+1
Empathetic attitude	0.998592	0.99864	0.980694	0.921718	0.939855
Knowledge sharing	0.271363	0.729995	0.955909	0.985379	0.999963
Deficiencies reduction	0.466068	0.955062	+1	0.959747	0.978548
Consistent performance	0.991175	0.999906	0.872784	0.783704	0.999877
Understanding self	0.965105	0.99685	0.999923	0.998822	0.978548
Skill-gap analysis	0.996681	0.988566	0.999249	+1	0.886965

Source: Primary data from field survey

Note: Pearson Correlation is used to explore the strength of the relationship between managing individual differences and developing proactive learning personalities. This gives an indication of both of direction (positive and negative) and the strength of relationship. The size of the value of Pearson Correlation (r) can range from 1.00 to 1.00. This value will indicate the strength of the relationship between two variables. A Correlation of 0 indicates no relationship at all, a correlation and value of 1.0 indicates a perfect positive correlation and value of -1.0 indicates a perfect negative correlation (r = 0.10 to r = 0.29 indicate small correlation, r = 0.30 to r = 0.49 indicate medium correlation, r = 0.50 to r = 1 indicate large correlation).

Factor represents the following: factor1 stands for Understanding Behavioral ramifications, factor2 presents learning necessitate, factor3 named for individual productivity, factor4 consists of competitive spirit and factor5 includes valuable presence of human resource at work.

Table 5 clearly shows the strong correlation between managing individual differences and developing proactive personalities. Strong correlation is observed among Creativity at work, Risk taking orientation, Deficiencies reduction and Skill-gap analysis (with +1 coeffients). Positive correlation is exists among Functional behaviors, Empathetic attitude, Consistent performance and understanding self. Medium correlation found between Work autonomy, Knowledge sharing. Factor 1 (Understanding behavioral ramifications) displayed a positive relation with all the personality inklings expect work autonomy (0.435932), knowledge sharing (0.271363) and deficiencies reduction (0.466068). Factor 2 (Learning necessitate) presented positive correlation with various personality dimensions. Factor 3 (Individual productivity) exhibited medium correlation with personality inkling risk taking orientation (0.475769). Factor 4 (Competitive spirit) demonstrated small correlation with personality factor work autonomy (0.178788) and Factor 5 (Valuable presence of human resource at work) exhibited a strong correlation with all personality inklings.

Major Findings

The following are key findings observed from above analysis:

1. The organizational factors like leadership, gender, team compositions, organizational culture, job role and expectations influences individual differences.
2. The impression of personality element on creativity, productivity, understanding the essence of individual differences is crucial in the context of organizational productivity.
3. Learning attitudes have been influenced by the personality factor. Proactive Learning helps the organizations in attaining sustainable competitive advantage; it happens only through developing proactive personalities. Proactive personalities, who are able to understand, assess and estimate exactly the past- present- anticipated future performance, job deficiencies, and required rate of performance.
4. The personality elements team efficacy, individual perceptions, self-monitoring, process improvement, role clarity and goal assessment are decisive in developing learning behaviors among human resources.
5. Employee performance in terms of productivity through learning attitudes lies with the competition acceptance levels, proactive appraisal mechanism, impression management, work environment, self-esteem, intuition, leadership, communication levels, divergent thinking, values and perceptions.
6. Majority of the respondents felt that there is strong correlation between managing individual differences and developing proactive learning personalities in this connection the human resources functional behaviors, creativity, work independence, risk taking propensity, empathetic attitudes towards understanding organizational issues are highly active workplace determinants.
7. The personality inklings like work autonomy, knowledge sharing, deficiencies reduction and risk taking orientation required unique attention; which are influencing more on learning attitudes of individuals.
8. Productivity element persuades the organizational progression, in particular knowledge sharing, deficiencies reduction and consistent performance facets associated with learning attitudes of employees.
9. Self-analysis is the best solution to major human resource issues; most of the examinees accepted its significance in personal and professional developments. Moreover personality notion is an ever changing factor in business competition arena.

10. Respondents expressed positively opinion towards improving proactive learning attitudes and recognized the need for devising a proactive learning schema to meet various organizational inflicts.
11. Overall the organizational expectation towards human resources is only one i.e. valuable presence, which is defined as having proactive learning behaviors, understanding organizational dynamics, managing risks, situational adapting and always trying to be unique in job performing and playing a vital role in organizational headway.

Strategic Imperatives

The following strategic imperatives are suggested to ensure proactive learning behaviors with augmented productivity under this typical business context:

- The human resources should realize the need for adopting proactive learning attitudes to meet critical organizational requirements.
- Re-engineering of organizational learning process is required, in this the individuals has to re-think about their perceptions towards the job essentials.
- Learning have direct impact on behavioral ramifications, productivity can be multiplied with valuable presence of employees at workplace.
- Continuous observation is required to reduce arena of individual differences by the superiors and self.
- Proactive Learning Schema is required to create proactive learning organizations. The detailed process of this schema is:
    i. Focusing more on right lining the individual differences.
    ii. Guiding behavioral deviations at work; rectifying misconceptions towards job, goals, role etc.
    iii. Determining performance metrics based on individual quantitative and qualitative outcomes with reference to organizational intensification.
    iv. High attention should be paid on creativity element, which is possible through the finding best ways of doing tasks and risk taking attitude.
    v. Asking the human resources to analyze themselves regarding to their professional performance, assessing rightly the deficiencies.
    vi. Functional behaviors are linked with the personality notion; accurate tuning behaviors of the individuals will results in improved recital.
    vii. Individual perceptions and values determine their job outcomes, so that the organizations ought to concentrate on continual improvement programs, goal-assessments and making them monitor themselves.

    viii. Work environment must be designed in such a way that setting proactive leaders, proactive appraisal mechanisms, adopting open communication system and accepting the levels of competition existed i.e. organizational and individual.

    ix. Impression management needed to be rightly devised to tackle various sensitive workplace issues of personality factor and

    x. Finally establishing the human resources as proactive learning personalities to widen scope of organizational development.

- Individual differences are needed to be properly managed through enhancing well-designed behaviors; making learning as a compulsory component to personal and professional improvements.
- Creating a knowledge sharing culture in the organizations through conducting sessions with experts, seniors, retired personnel and working employees who are rated as extraordinary performers.
- Encouraging human resources to handle the risky decisions at work. Giving work independence with having frequent work reviews meetings.
- Maintaining proactive performance management system to ensure continuous performance improvement programs by which employees can reduce their various deficiencies at workplace.
- Shaping Behavior may be used an effective tool to handle individual differences. It is a systematically reinforcing each successive step that moves an individual closer to the desired response. Positive reinforcements (appraisals) and Negative reinforcements (punishments) should be adopted as per the personality management requirements.
- Teams effectiveness can be improved only by spotlighting the individual echelon; group cohesiveness, innovations, fault repairs, process improvements lies with understanding the quintessence of reshaping individual differences.

Scope for further Research

The present study is limited to assessing the influence of individual differences on learning attitudes with augmented productivity. Therefore, there is abundant scope for exploration in this area, like the following:

- Impact of individual differences on leadership transformations.
- Individual differences influence on creative task accomplishments.
- Role of individual differences on team-efficacy: A Personality Analysis.
- A study on impact of empathetic attitude on lining individual differences.
- Managing individual differences a panorama to transform organizational impressions on diversified workforce.

Conclusion

Personality element determines many key issues at workplace; if it is properly managed the results may be beyond measure. Proactive learning personalities create sustainable, unique, zero-competition threat, endless meticulousness organizations. Proactive learning is possible only through structuring the individual differences. The dynamic business environment presents many novel challenges and issues in front of the organizations and individuals; to solve these enigmas the indispensable module is only proactive learning.

References

Aguilar-Alonso, A. (1996). *Personality and creativity*. Personality and Individual Differences, 21, 959–969.

Batey, M., & Furnham, A. (2006). *Creativity, intelligence, and personality: A critical review of the scattered literature*. Genetic, Social and General Psychology Monographs, 132, 455–929.

Bolin, A., U., & Neuman, G., A., (2006). *Personality, Process, and Performance in Interactive Brainstorming Group*. Journal of Business and Psychology, 20(4), pp. 565-585.

Burke, L., A., & Witt, L., A., (2004). *Personality and High-Maintenance Employee Behavior*. Journal of Business and Psychology,18(3), pp. 349-363.

Chamorro-Premuzic, T. (2007). *Personality and individual differences*. Oxford, UK: Blackwell.

Chamorro-Premuzic, T., & Reichenbacher, L. (2008). *Effects of personality and threat of evaluation on divergent and convergent thinking*. Journal of Research in Personality, 42, 1095–1101.

Chauhan, D., & Chauhan, S., P., (2006). *Personality at Workplace*. Indian Journal of Industrial Relations, 41(3), pp. 357-375.

Colquitt, J, Le-Pine, J, & Wesson, M. (2009). *Organizational Behavior; improving performance and commitment in the workplace*, New York, McGraw-Hill, Irwin.

Davis Mkoji & Dr. Damary Sikalieh (2012).*The Influence of Personality Dimensions on Organizational Performance*.International Journal of Humanities and Social Science Vol. 2 No. 17; September 2012.

Dr.Y.Subbarayudu & G.V.Chandra Mouli (2012). *The Dynamics of Personality Traits on Individual Performance – Its Impact and Influential Analysis at Workplace*. International Journal of Decision Making in Management Volume 1, Issue 2, pp.12-20, October-December 2012.

Esque, T.J, & Gilmore, E.R (2003). *Making an Impact; Building a Top Performing Organization from the Bottom up*. Performance Improvement, Volume 42, Issue 1, pp. 47–49, January 2003.

Fred Luthans (2003). *Organizational Behavior*. McGraw-Hill International Edition, India.

Furnham, A. (2008). *Personality and intelligence at work*. London: Routledge.

Furnham, A., Batey, M., Anand, K., & Manfield, J. (2008*). Personality, hypomania, intelligence and creativity*. Personality and Individual Differences, 44, 1060–1069.

Gerhardt, M., Bryan, A. & Newman, R.W. (2009).*Understanding the impact of proactive personality on job performance: the roles of tenure and self-management*, Journal of Leadership & Organizational studies.

Guilford, J. P. (1967). *The nature of human intelligence*. New York: McGraw-Hill.

Gumusluoglu, L., Ilsev, A., (2009). *Transformational leadership, creativity, and organizational innovation*. Journal of Business Research, 62, pp.461–473.

Kim, T., Hon, A., & Crant, J. J. (2009). *Proactive Personality, Employee Creativity, and Newcomer Outcomes: A Longitudinal Study*. Journal of Business & Psychology, 24(1), 93-103.

R.N.Taylor and M.D.Dunnette (1974). *"Influence of Dogmatism, Risk-Taking Propensity, and Intelligence on Decision-Making Strategies for a Sample of Industrial Managers*. Journal of Applied Psychology, August 1974, pp.420-23.

Stephen p.robbins & Seema Sanghi (2006). *Organizational Behavior*. Dorling Kindersley(India) Pvt. Ltd., licenses of Pearson Education in South Asia.

Vincent, A., Decker, B., & Mumford, M. (2002). *Divergent thinking, intelligence and expertise*. Creativity Research Journal, 19, 163–178.

Wagner, J.A, & Hollenbeck J.R. (1998).*Organizational Behavior; Securing Competitive Advantage*, (ed), New Jersey, Prentice Hall.

Westerman, J.W. & Simmons, B.L. (2007). *The effects of work environment on the personality-performance relationship: an exploratory study*. Journal of Managerial Issues: pp.339-97.

YOUR KNOWLEDGE HAS VALUE

- We will publish your bachelor's and master's thesis, essays and papers

- Your own eBook and book - sold worldwide in all relevant shops

- Earn money with each sale

Upload your text at www.GRIN.com
and publish for free